The Pain of Love

And Other Minor Works Of Poetry

Taneisha Grace

AuthorHouse™
1663 Liberty Drive
Bloomington, IN 47403
www.authorhouse.com
Phone: 1-800-839-8640

© 2010 Taneisha Grace. All rights reserved.

No part of this book may be reproduced, stored in a retrieval system, or transmitted by any means without the written permission of the author.

First published by AuthorHouse 1/18/2010

ISBN: 978-1-4490-5411-3 (e)
ISBN: 978-1-4490-5410-6 (sc)
ISBN: 978-1-4490-6859-2 (hc)

Library of Congress Control Number: 2009914360

Printed in the United States of America
Bloomington, Indiana

This book is printed on acid-free paper.

Dedicated to my family who pushed me, the people who hurt me and God for giving me the strength to turn my pain into creativity.

Four Letter Word

Love, yes that great word divine,
The word that escapes your mouth at the wrong time,
And sometimes it feels right but your heart doesn't
feel it to and you get ahead of yourself before your
mind can give you the right words to speak,
Shortly afterward you feel weak in the knees,
And your brain begins to freeze,
As you're the who said the "thing"
That four letter word that means so much,
That holds the very key to everyone's soul,
The only word in the word that can make you cry out
and give up everything you once held pure inside,
And if it means that much then you let it take your life,
Love that word that conquers all hurts from the past,
And can make you give your very last,
It whispers I am here forever by your side,
And tells you to let go,
It tells you to be whole again and to love once more,
To forget about your past and build again,
It sweeps you off your feet, once more into
the clouds of joy and no weeps,
And although you want to let it show that you think
they are amazing and you'll love them forever,
You know you and don't know how
to pull your heart out of it's
surrounding leather case,
So instead you try again, instead of running away,
And your heart is restored to it's original holding place….

Heart & Soul

Loving you with all my heart and soul,
Giving myself to you of nothing less than whole,
Wanting you more each day because
you are the one for me,
Loving you as we know love birds are true and free,
Loving each other is what we do,
No matter how much I may make you mad
or disappoint you,
Wanting more of your love each day,
As your attitude makes me sway, more
and more your way,
Loving you with all my heart and soul,
Because nothing else doth my soul long for,
Than to love you, yes all of you, mind,
body and soul, more and more….

Never Thought

Never thought I could get so high
just to get right back down,
To get so excited just to fall to the ground,
To feel so loved just to be left alone,
To plan and get so much just to go through the cold alone,
Just be left at the alter with nothing but the same sad song,

Never thought that day would come when
my so-called "Prince" would come,
Just to be left in the pouring rain,
Just to be left brokenhearted and feeling so much pain,
To feel high above the earth to have
to once again face reality,
That in this life there nothing out there for me,

Never thought that he could be the
one in the midst of the night,
That would tear my hert up as soon as he mends it,
That would fil me joy and replace it with more anxiety,
That would fill it with love and throw
it away piece by piece,
Never thought…

Never thought, should've known, and now I sit with tears
rolling down my face saying I should've known all along…

Actions W/Out Regret... You...

You throw me off because you feel down,
But I thought I was the one to lift you up when you were down, are down or when you're feeling low to the ground,
Thought I was the one who was suppose to help you through it and yet you
treat me as if I'm some sideline chick,

You push me away because you don't
know how to speak to me,
But what, do I not have feelings too?
The one to pick you up when your days not going right or when you're feeling blue,
Am I not the one that can help you get through?

You expect me to be able to read your mind,
Yet you call me your wife and I'm always trying to be there for you right on time,
And you can forsake me without a heartbeat on drop of a dime,
And then want me to forget when that history is still apart of the present time,

Thought I was your dime, thought I was your
world, and now I'm suppose to know how you feel
when every time I ask you say that you're okay,
I ask the same question almost every hour of everyday,
The way you treat me makes my actions sway
from left to right from day to day,
    When I'm suppose to be your world and you treat me
      like some random girl as if I don't have pain too, so
      why can't we help each other make it through????

You, I & Love....

I love you because you are never willing to change for those around,
On the phone, or face to face playing around on the floor or on the ground,
Talk is cheap and love can be faked,
Day by day, night by night,
Even if you pretend to be a prince in the darkest of the nights,
Love is love and yours is different makes me feel so indifferent,
Every time you whisper, every time I shiver, and everyday when I lie awake and think of what's to come of this day,
Is forever long enough to love you and only you?
Will we to each other forever be of only love and truth?
Will I choose you and only you? And you do the same for me?
Or will there be a twist In time where we are two souls in search of the same thing,
Something real, something true because of the games we dealt,
Either way in search of something that's forever and real,
Although what we have is real enough,
But will it end and please the crowd of hostess waiting for us let it seize,
Or will we engulf In love and passion forever more,
I'd like to think of a world containing only you and I but that is a mere fantasy and never could one be reality,
So save your breathe and mellow speech's for

the crowd because they miss you too,
But can they ever love you and give up
their life for you as I would,
    Maybe what we have is just good for you, not
      good enough and never will be enough….

-Power of Love-

Reflecting upon life I never realized how much
I had grown or changes over time,
How much I had achieved and grown to
be the woman that I am today,
I never thought that love could hold so
much power over me in life,
Hell I never thought love would come,
Not once to be so non-transparent
upon hitting the scorching sun,
And so translucent with the brightness of
the moonlight. It's amazing how hope withers away in thinking of change for a phase,
Not expressing how it feels in the cruelest of ways,
Sometimes things can take me by surprise but
to know someone had loved was worth more
than a life full of surprise after sunrise,
 So I begin to think if having faith and hope might
be too much, too extreme to make you see the things
that I could see or know the things I know,
Or just to be patient and wait not knowing what's next,
Thinking about what the future could be,
                And not knowing exactly love would
                      ever have in store for me….

-Damaged Heart-

Day by day he repairs a damaged heart,
Mending together the puzzles of a broken soul,
Both shattered into pieces by things done and said,
By actions and words unheard of,
Hopefully he won't hurt me like those of my past,
Because then history would repeat itself,
Then I'd be mad because I let my
heart out of it's cage of cold,
And now heat my soul would pour,
Of tears of sorrow and pain and scorn,

Day by day he repairs a damaged heart,
Wasn't sure at first but now I know he cares,
Every time I turn around on my face there lies a smile,
Even when the rain was pouring he
was there to hold me through,
Making the sun shine although it was dark around,
Waiting all night and letting the mu-
sic be a soft and gentle sound,
While teaching me again what it felt to be cared about,
Causing me to dream of him throughout the night,
Mending a damaged heart and holding me tight,
      Works just fine, I think now I'll be alright…

~Unconditional Love~

I'd marry you because your love is unconditional,
You take me to higher places than no other has before,
The connection we have, no words can describe,
It wasn't about a matter of time,
It has a place in the normal love race,
But what we have is not normal,
But unheard of in this world,
Thinking outside to box to please each other so true,
So I begin to ask myself what can I do for you?

I'd marry you because your love is unconditional,
But would you marry me too?
You guarantee blue skies and I promise not to make you mad,
To always be your light when you're angry or sad,
Just your love is all I ask unconditionally forever and not just know,
And I promise the same in return,
Because I love you so much I cry for you,
        I love you unconditionally, no lie, just
            truth, that I'll always love you!

Most Men in my Life

Most men in my life hurt me,
To the point that I am angry,
Feeling alone and abused,
Feeling mistreated and misused,

Most men in my life have cheated,
Traded me in for a son,
Got what they could get and in the
end left me out-run,

Most men in my life lie,
And expect me to apologize,
For the anger that I feel,
For the attitude I dish,
Just to do what you did to me,
See how it's planted so deep as a seed,

Most men in my life loose my trust,
And if I trust past a week,
It ain't luck,
It's God's mercy and his grace because He knows my heart,
So fragile and gentle, that's just a start,

Most men in my life cut me up and spit me out,
And if you ask why am I so cold,
I'll tell you that I have a gentle soul….

My Motivation

You are the motivation and inspiration behind my writing,
The love that flows beyond my songs,
The memories that overrun,
You are my motivation,
The one who speaks for me in my time of need,
The only one I see,
The only one I wish to be with,
Floating above the clouds,
The one to be with during a drought,
You are my motivation,
The strength behind my inspiration,
The one who captivates who I really am,
Who knows my emotions and understands me,
Not just when I'm angry but the all around me,
So can I tell you how you are my motivation and inspiration behind my writings????

Tired

Tired of being invisible to you
when all do is love you and
show that I care and
Want to be with you standing
by your side while you running the streets,
Have I reached the point to where
I can't take being invisible any more to you,
So this is where I draw the line
And call it through....

Everyone wants Love

Everyone wants someone to love,
Someone to hold when nights are cold,
I want to be comforted, I want to be held,
I want to leave a legacy that my love won't forget,
And to give child in the midst of it,
To be held just because to be told I love you just because of who I am and not because of what I can give,
Everyone wants to be loved,
In some way or fashion,
So will I be loved by a man outside my own house,
Taken upon a hill just to see a beautiful view,
Just because of love, just for being me,
Is that enough to find the love at which I seek???

How Can I still Love You???

I'm thinking about you day and night,
Even though I have a boo,
Wondering if things changed so much
that you don't think of me too,
While at the same time I ask my-
self, how can I still love you?
It's been maybe two years since we last dated,
But I think of you like crazy, nothing unordinary,
Try to get rid of you, try to move forward,
So again I ask myself, how can I still love you?
Am I crazy or just a fool?
It could never be just us two,
You've moved on and I have tried,
But always end back at this point in time,
I ask this question again and again,
How is it possible,
Why, is it karma, chemistry, because it's not obsession,
How do I, and how can I STILL LOVE YOU???

Serious Love

What scares me the most is that you're
the first guy that was ever serious about loving me,
So I seek answers within myself
and guidance from my council,
Because I'm lost and confused,
I don't know what to say,
I don't know what to do,
Because I'm loving you so much
without knowing what to do with myself,
Waiting for you patiently daily
just to see your caring face,
What scares me is that you're the best ever,
And I'm not sure if you think of
me the way that I think of you,
So I'm scared because not once has
any man loved me like you do,
Not once have they cared as to
keep our love strong and true…

Unfathomable

Unfathomable thoughts unspoken in my mind,
Make me think of you more while time steadily creeps by,
I picture you, I picture me, I pic-
ture us and hope it's meant to be,
I go into the water picturing you holding me,
Swimming into the deep depths of the sea,
Asking what of this life,
Of what is exactly meant to be,
Am I to ever overcome my fear and speak to you alone,
Or will my soul wither away from the same love sick-song,

Unfathomable thoughts unspoken of in time,
Doth invade my mind while I'm grasping on to you and
only because all my thoughts concern you and more of you,
Your smile so bright, so intrigu-
ing, that it literally pulls me in,
Your eyes maybe deceiving as he looks at
mw and they call me nearer to him,
His touch, so soft and gentle,
That they send chills down my spine as he grasp me to
bring my head closer to his chest to hold me close,
His kiss, of sweet scent of strawberries upon
his breath I inhale as we meet lip to lip,
While he tightens his grasp as in say-
ing I'm your's for eternity,
I am yours and I care for you, not him but
I do and you know that I love you,

Unfathomable thoughts unspoken in my mind,
Unspeakable in life,
  Makes me realize I you too and more day in day out but we know we must fight it and go our separate lives….

-Matter-

Why does it matter that
I'm in love with you,
When you're not in love with me?
If time is what you want then by all means,
Just don't keep me waiting too long,
Might disappear into another's arms,
As so you have thought before
never realizing that I always thought of you,
Why does it matter that I'm
in love with you or that I'm
tired of running from what
I know of love to be true,
Always making me smile,
turning pitch black days sky blue,
Thinking of no man but you and only you,
I cry myself to sleep at night
because I long to hear your voice, I long for you,
Wondering if you'll ever speak to me again,
Or want to be with me too,
But those thoughts come and
go swiftly as I know that they
will never happen or ever become true,
Why does it matter to me so
much and not to you at all,
Maybe this is why LOVE is my downfall….

Forget me: Forget me Not

Forget me, forget me not, forget me, forget me not,
Are words of a child's game,
Now these very words are what cause me to go insane,
Forget me, forget me not, is like say-
ing I love you but I don't,
Pulling back the reigns to let feelings just cease be-
fore going blind or going into love too deep,
Forget me, forget me not, like calling forth my
heart only to walk, stumper and tread over it,
While it hurts inside and makes me sick,
So you say forget me and I say forget me
not, because I'm in love with you,
Even though you didn't love me back,
even though skies weren't blue,
Forget me, forget me not, forget me, forget me
not as I still long for your warm embrace,
I dare you to forgive me and forget me not....

-Remind Me-

Your smile reminds me of cuddling while the rain is falling,
Your eyes remind me of the summers cool breeze,
Constantly telling me that I can be loved, that I am free,
Your grasp and hold reach to the depths of my soul,
Making me feel renewed, making me feel whole,
Your touch sends chills of sensation and satisfaction down my spine,
Knowing you could be mine for all time,
Your personality reminds me of no one because you're unique and special in everyway,
Warming my heart from our very first date,
You just for being who you are remind me of beautiful things that make me smile inside,
Hoping I can capture your heart and more
than just for a little while…..

.....Time....

Now here and comes where the problem lies me
wanting to wait and you wanting to rush time,
Thinking I won't be here forever that's
the doubt within my mind,
While loving each other is what we do in and out of time,
I'll be yours forever as long as you want to be mine and
don't doubt my love for you, no not ever one time,
Cause what we have is not ordinary but
something sweet and divine,
Now forgive me for wanting to wait cause nothing can break our love, no not this time,
Now the settlement is to wait for that one
kiss when everything has sealed,
Knowing that no matter what that
my broken heart you healed,
And knowing that our love and love at first sight is real,
And that no matter what either of us say or do,
The love we share is very true and goes beyond the words of I do and I do too…

Pass

Pass death, pass life til the end of earth's flight,
Pass trees, pass mountains, sky high
and depths of the ocean floor,
Pass your blood line, pass our family trees,
I love you more than deep of deeps,
Pass rain drops that never stop,
Pass heartbeats that never give up,
Pass tears flowing down out faces,
Pass bonds that are never broken,
I love you more than deep of deeps,
Pass bondage or being free,
Pass life and liberty, pass slavery in history,
I love you more than deep of deeps,
Pass never-ending games, pass ever growing seeds,
Pass beating heartbeats of the meek,
Pass anguish and fear of those that live miserably,
Grasping on to anger and hurt,
Pass the depth of roots of trees,
I love you deeper and more than the deep of deeps....

How Do I....

How do I say I love you,
Without saying goodbye,
How do I say I want to be with you,
Without telling you why,
How do I say I want you near without
Putting in words above all else
how I really feel,
How do I say I want you,
Without scaring you away,
How do I say you mean the world to me,
Without a smile and tears rolling down my face,
How do I say you're the one without
being scared you might run away,
How do I say I love you,
Without saying goodbye,
How do I say I want you for more
than just a little while....

-Remind Me-

Your smile reminds me of cuddling
while the rain is falling,
Your eyes remind me of summer's cool
breeze constantly telling me I can be
loved and I am free,
Your grasp and hold reach
to the depths of my soul
Making me feel renewed,
making me feel whole,
Your touch sends chills
down my spine,
And knowing you could
be mine for all time,
Your personality reminds
me of no one
because you're unique and
special in everyway,
Warming my heart from
our very first date,
You just for being who you are
remind me of beautiful things t
hat make me smile inside,
Hoping I can capture your heart and
more than just for a little while…

~You Seem~

You seem to know what's in my heart
without having known me long,
You seem to know when something's
on my mind an so far you're never wrong,
You seem to sense my wants,
my needs although I think it strange,
Because no man but you has never
has to ask me for my name,
You seem to understand me in
ways I can't explain,
Nothing but love flows from me to you,
In ways we can't maintain,
All the factors of love that
makes you go insane,
You seem to know me almost
better than I know myself,
You seem to know what's in my heart
without having known my heart long,
But it feels like it's been longer than an eternity….

~More~

I love you so don't rush my love
is here to forever stay,
Being confirmed with God
more each and everyday,
So as we take this short time
compared to the rest of our lives,
To get in plenty of qt time,
While reading each other's expressions
and flying inside our minds,
I want you to know I'll love you
for the rest of our lives,
Only changing to love you more
than I did before no less,
But love so much more from
now until forever more,
I love you and that will never change
for what we have is not a temporary
marriage but an everlasting must....

~I Love You Because~

I love you because you're here,
I love you because you're amazing,
Because you're different and
true to who you are,
You make me laugh,
You make me smile,
Even as the rain falls from the sky
And we sit staring into each other's eye's,
I'm falling in love with you,
Each and every time,
I love you because you're not with me
Because of what I have to give,
But because you care for me too,
Staying with me til I'm asleep and making
Sure I'm good after a bad dream,
I love you because you're not all about you,
You're sincere and kind and we haven't known
Each other for a long time,
But if we stopped and pushed rewind,
Together we've had so much time,
Some laughs, and some shared deep pains,
About the things that burdened, or burdens us,
And I have you for it all, love was made for us,
And even though it's cold, I have you
And you have I too hold so in actuality

We are never cold,
Just two souls coming together,
To make what was broken souls now again whole,
I love you because of what you give me mentally,
I love you for who you are and the things you do,
I love you because our love is of faith and truth…

How Do You

How do you tell someone you want them there?
How do you tell them that before you were scared?
How do you tell them now how you feel?
How will they know that this is real?
How do you take back what you said?
How do you reel them in with no bread?
How do you tell him that's he's gentle
without raising a red flag?
How do you go and change the past?
How do you let them know that they make you smile?
How do you tell them that it was just a mistake,
How at the time you didn't have the courage to be brave,
How now you still want them in every way?
How do you tell them, that you miss them every second and every minute of everyday????

Different

He's different from any other and not like every other wanna be fake brother,
Doesn't try to spit game,
He's himself and around his boys the same,
May show out in public to make me laugh
But still he maintains,
Hummm, he misses me as much as I miss him,
And when we kiss there is fire in his lips, his veins,
But he above all others, he keeps his peace and he maintains,
He, he is different like a new melody in my head that gives me peace of mind and peace in my sleep,
He is everything that other guys should want to be,
He keeps my mind running,
But he also helps me sleep,
He erases all past tragedies,
He's different indeed,
But he is the definition of what other young brothers should want to be
Himself and no added preservatives are needed,
Himself, how all other guys should want to be…

Can't Stop

Can't stop thinking about you,
So I write about you,
All I dream about is loving you,
Being with you for an eternity would
be my dreams,
Being with you in your arms,
I feel so much peace,
The happiness you're brought me,
No one can compare,
The chills up and down my spine,
No one dared,
You are you and nothing less,
So much more of myself I want to give,
Loving you and you knowing that
I am for real,
Can't stop thinking about you,
So I smile every time I see you,
And I hope you'll forever feel the same as I do,
When it comes to wanting you to love me
as I want to love you…

However you choose to Refer...

They wanna sex me and say that they're loving me,
Maybe it's my imagination, maybe it's just a dream,
Dudes, males, thugs wanna be's,
however you choose to refer,
Always claim I'll be there for you and I'll always love you,
When truly I'm only holding myself down,
When they tell you I love you just to sleep with you,
Tell you everything you want to hear just to be with you,
And so easily with material things and
friends, they replace you,
Dudes, males, thug wanna be's and such,
however you choose to refer,
They only come to permanently break your
heart and tear you apart,
And soon after your heart has been broken many times,
You'll be singing the same sad song...

Slow Down

I TELL MYSELF TO SLOW DOWN SO I WON'T
SINK IN QUICKSAND,
BUT I WANT TO KNOW WHAT IT'S
LIKE TO KNOW LOVE AGAIN,
I WATCH HIS EYES PIERCE MINE,
AS WE HOLD EACH OTHER IN TIME,
PASSING FORWARD TOGETHER
THROUGH EACH SINGLE LINE,
OF THE POETRY I'VE WRITTEN
FROM THOSE OF MY PAST LIFE,
I TELL MYSELF TO SLOW DOWN SO I WON'T
SINK IN QUICKSAND,
BUT JUST AS I PREPARE TO LEAVE,
I SEE HIM SITTING UPON A TREE
SINGING SWEET MELODIES,
OF LIFE WITH HIM BEING NOTHING BUT FREE,
SO I ASK MYSELF WHAT IS THERE TO FEAR,
BUT STILL I SLOW DOWN THAT WAY
I MAY KEEP SOME SANITY….

My Way…

To hold you through the night would make my day,
Guess everything can't always be my way,
Just to wake up with you next to me at my side,
Would've been nice,
Although, I never tried because of my own pride,
Guess that's life, we kiss, you leave,
And come back the next day,
But I guess that's how it ends in your way and not way,
Or my ending of the perfect romantic day…

Heartbroken & Scorn...

Sick of giving all that I can give with nothing but scorn in return
Filling with anger, hurt and pain,
An idea to shut off the world,
Cause love takes control and I begin to let go off the hurt and pain from before only to be left again,
Heartbroken and scorn,
I say love you, you say you love me to,
But actions speak louder than words and yours don't show that you do,
It shows of what you want me to do for you and how you want me to treat you,
But I'm staying up late cause I got the I love you blues only to be torn and driven,
Left once again heartbroken and scorn,
I give all that I can give and you take,
All I wanted was your complete love for at least a day or mybe a little while,
To know that you care about if I smile,
Start from scratch is what I begin to do,
Only to be heartbroken and scorn of a heart that's already broken and torn...

Too Much To Ask…

Been hurt so much and they always say they care,
But they know that they will never be there,
To hold my hand through the night,
Or to hold me while I'm asleep,
They'll only be there temporarily,
Never wanting something that'll last forever,
Been broken down one relationship after the other,
With nothing but disappointments and only temporary joy,
Got me wondering was there ever any-
thing between us called love?
Tossed and driven in a love ocean so wide,
Hoping and wishing for that right guy,
Slow to anger me and always makes me happy,
Is it too much to ask for cause right now
I'm not asking for marriage,
Been there, done that, I don't want to go back,
I just want someone that's real…
Is that too much to ask????

His Eyes, His voice, Our Love

His eyes hold so much compassion,
One that is everlasting,
His face shows so much emotion of you
look beyond his looks,
The pain, the hurt, the things that,
Make him not just a man but a gentleman,
His voice holds so much sincerity,
So gentle, kind and one that makes me smile,
One that listens, gives advice and is not
Around for just a little while,
He is real and our love is oh so real,
Regardless os what others think,
They can't understand our level,
Til they've been in out shoes of how we feel what we feel,
And how we do the things we do,
When above all else, loving each other is what we do….

Love Flees

Love flees from me when I'm in reach of it,
It peaks it's head for a minute just to hurt me,
Love knows no bounds and will never love me,
Never know me because when I'm near it always flees,
Love flees my right as I encounter it never stopping to love only to befriend me,
Will love ever grow to know me or love me?
Companionship and love go hand in hand,
Will I ever have love without my
heart sinking in quicksand,
Love will never know me because it flees from me,
So are you too a close up of love that
should flee from my sight too??
Or the on who will turn my rainy days to sunlight
and my midnight skies to summer's sky blue????

Why Can't I???

Why can't I be loved like everyone else,
Loving each other for better or worse,
Needing nothing less or anyone else,
Why can't I be loved and held on to like I
'm his last dime,
Wanting me and only me throughout
forever in time,
Because what we'd have would be
So divine,
Why can't love come my way,
And be with me forever to stay,
Why can't I too be loved for me
And not just for my looks,
Why can't I be loved like everyone else,
Why can't I be loved just like you do????

That Guy

That guy to hold you through the night,
In the right position, nice and tight,
That guy to make you feel special inside,
To help you to restore your pride,
That guy that makes the darkness disappear,
The one to spend a night with, without any fears,
That guy that makes you smile with every word,
Speaking to you in a love language you've never heard,
That guy that says I won't hurt you,
The one to be with through and through,
That guy that tells you, you're the one,
That takes you when it's cold and you're
The only one he wants to hold,
That guy to say everything will be okay,
Just you rest and leave it God's hands,
And know that He will make a way,
That guy that comforts you when you want to cry,
And will try to cheer you up with questions,
Pity, or strife,
That guy to make you feel alright,
Meeting your mother and knowing to have
no worries or frets,
She likes him already although he doesn't know it yet,
That guy that proposes because he
loves you and he wants to,
That guy is perfect simply because he's saying I love you….

Where Your Heart Is...

Go where your heart is,
Don't let it slip away,
Do what you have to do and
Say what you have to say,
Don't let your true love
JUST SLIP AWAY…

Maybe hard to get true love back,
Maybe hard to fight for it,
Maybe hard to see the light at first,
You may not know it was true love
til you have someone else,

It's so amazing love,
My friend says go where your heart is,
Don't let love slip away,
Do what you got to do and
Say what you have to say,
But by all means,
Don't let true love slip away….

Afraid You're Gonna Forget...

Afraid you're gonna forget about me,
So now I began to feel lonely,
As if you're not even there,
Afraid you're going to get famous
and forget about me,
And just call me up whenever you need me,
My love, my one and only,
I'm afraid we'll be too distanced
From one another,
So you will replace me with another,
Afraid you're gonna forget about me…
afraid of being lonely…

So Sick

So sick of love like repeat melodies of pain and hurt and sorrow

and grief,

So sick falling in love and left standing in the rain,

You tell me you love me knowing it's only temporary that last

no more than five or ten minutes,

So sick of love like my favorite love tracks cause they only make

me reflect on why I love you or used to love you and only you,

Leaving me for her and I gave my heart and soul,

Now you leave me standing alone in the cold,

So sick of love and everything it entails because when I say I

love you there is a bond I cherish,

And forever want to hold,

Not to be left crying for my heart to turn black and cold,

So I'm sick of love, so you can have it,

And I hope you never feel the same way I do,

Now watch me turn your sky blue days to midnight blue….

Unknown

I have been hurt so many times before you,
I don't know what I am suppose to do,
I don't know I can live without you,
So I sit inside feeling so blue,
Can I have love that will remain forever true,
Can I have love that won't change for their friends,
Can I have love that makes me feel whole again,
Can we go away for more than a spell,
Just the two of us leaving this life of hell,
I have been hurt many times before you,
I sit thinking what wrong did I do,
So now I'm lost and I'm so confused,
Living alone trying once more to live,
Living alone with a broken heart again,
I have been hurt many times before you,
I sit alone crying inside,
Trying not to let my guard down past my pride,
So I think to myself again is this the
type of life I am destined to,
Alone, broken hearted, misused and abused,
So what on earth am I suppose to do?
I have been hurt so many times before you,
So lonely I sit thinking so confused, living this life with no mate by my side,

So again I sit and cry,
I have been hurt,
I have been showed,
Just like a past,
What am I to gain,
Turn away from love cause it hurt so much,
I have been hurt so much before you,
So if you have to leave, then do what you have to do....

Love, Love

I LOVE, LOVE AS IT LOVES ME,
EVEN WHEN IT DOESN'T SEEM TO LOVE ME
TOO,
I LOVE, LOVE THROUGH MIDNIGHT SKIES AND
BLUE SKIES THROUGH AND THROUGH,
IRREGARDLESS OF HOW I FEEL AND EVEN
WHEN I WANT TO
FEEL HAPPINESS AS LOVE FEELS IT TOO,
TO BE LOVED COMPLETELY BY LOVE
AND NOTHING ELSE,
TO FEEL LOVE RUN THROUGH MY BODY
AS OTHERS FEEL IT TOO,
KNOWING THAT IT LOVES ME AS MUCH
AS I LOVE HIM TO,
I LOVE, LOVE? AS IT LOVES ME OR MORE
SO I LOVE IT MORE,
THAN TO BE FEELING LONELY OR JUST DO DIS-
AAPOINTED TO THE CORE,
I LOVE, LOVE AS IT ONCE LOVED ME,
BUT FOR SOME REASON IT ONCE AGAIN
FLEES FROM ME,
TRANQULIZING MY FEELINGS TO
SOME STABILTY,
FLEEING AT EVERY CORNER AND

MAKING MY LEGS GO WEAK,
I LOVE, LOVE AS IT LOVES ME,
SO I THINK OF DAYS AS NIGHTS AND
NIGHTS AS DAYS,
AS I WATCH TIME FADE AWAY,
SO I LOVE, LOVE AS IT LOVES ME,
TO LOVE, LOVE AND BE FREE
ABOVE ALL FREES....

So See Through

So fragile, so dense, so see through,
That's how I feel when guys look around from me to you,
When they look at me as if I'm a prize,
Then they look at my heart as if it don't ex-
ist in the palm of their hand,
So they toss it, not knowing exactly where it may land,
Just to then make their move upon me,
Saying I'll always be there for you,
As they prepare to go inside,
While underneath I feel like I've lost
all dignity and self pride,
So fragile, so dense, so see through,
That's how I feel when they look from me to you,
Apart of me that stains blood red of an-
ger and vengeance for days,
Never seeming to care as they go through
the motions of caring each day,
Sweet, I love your kisses upon my cheek,
While upon the windowsill lays my heart,
He comes and goes right behind me, clean-
ing and knocking it off,
And slowly I begin to fall back like the times before,
In my bed I lay awake crying hoping to have my heart back,
In my hands to have that perfect person,
So fragile, so dense, so see through to them,
They hold within the palm of their hands but
they can not see so they toss it away,
This fragile, dense and so see through part
of me that's all just a big dream…..

Shattered

My heart was shattered and is shattered
into a million pieces,
And constantly I try to hope for a man
to mend it,
That thing so pure that holds the holds the
key to my soul,
That makes me, breaks me, or makes
me feel whole,
Can't be broken anymore or shattered
never the less cause I
Give up on love, because my best interest,
that's the best,
Cause no longer do I want my heart
mended just to be shattered again,
My heart has shattered been shattered, mended and
broken all over again,
My heart was shattered and is shattered
into a million pieces,
So am I the fool that keeps breaking it,
By always letting someone come in to
mend is and it be broken again,
It becomes frozen and fragile left
alone in the cold,
Becomes heated and warm as in summer
waiting for a love that's bold,

Trying to do it's best with every man
that comes it's way,
Only to be left hurting and crying again for days,
Asking will I ever find someone to
love me just for me,
Or will I constantly be a laughing stock of
wanting the man of dreams….

Love Is....

Love is gentle, patient and kind,
It is not hurt, jealousy or pride,
Love is not perfect,
One would never be worth it,
Love is an indefinite emotion,
Although sometimes it's like a roller coaster,
Love is understanding,
Not mis-leading or mis- guiding,
Love is taking the extra mile,
It even requires sacrifice,
Love is more than admiration of
demise or a strong affection,
It requires your all and asks your best,
Love is more then adoration,
Looks should never be something that
comes into phase,
Love requires a strong foundation,
And no matter what it must remain unchangeable,
Love is everything you want it to be and more,
Love is what everyone wants and longs for....

Two Souls

Two souls wondering earth broken-hearted,
Now encounter one another,
Two souls wondering the earth,
Wondering if they'll ever love again,
Trying to find reason within the world again,
Never hurting their mates while they
live in a world with sin,
Two souls now meet and try to join within,
Two souls try to mend once broken hearts
to make themselves whole again…

I Love You More

I love you more today than I did yesterday,
You came and took the pain away,
I love you more today than I did five days ago,
You came and you made me feel whole,
I love you more today that I did a week ago,
You came and made a still waters flow,
I love you more today that I did two weeks ago,
You came and gave me your heart and now two souls
are whole,
I love more today than I did a month ago,
For then I barely knew you but now we are here,
I love you more today that I did years ago because
When you walked into my life and immediately you
filled every broken hole....

You Are...

You are the one and only,
You are the one for me,
You are the one who fills my
dreams and my destiny,
No other love can compare
our chemistry,
I who you are,
I love how you make me feel,
I love you and this, no lie but truth,
You are the one and only,
You are the one for me,
You are the one who fills my
Dreams and my destiny,
And I'll love you forever, til eternity....

Irresistible

You could call him irresistible,
He had a stare that would pull you in,
And constantly it would make your head spin,
The way he talked would make you want to
sit and stare awhile,
He talked to you not thinking about time,
Just him in your life could make the sun,
You could call him irresistible,
The way he held you close,
The way he's talk late at night,
Gently while putting you to sleep,
Telling you things so sweetly,
That only causes you to have just sweet dreams,
You could call him irresistible with that smile,
That just highlights your day,
Makes you wonder what he's up too,
When you're not together,
Makes you get that chill and every time
your eyes intertwine,
You could call him irresistible,
Although he's just a friend,
Tell him how much you really feel,
Because you know he'll be there til the end,
Simply because you'll always be nothing more than friends…

Melt

Wanting to be loved, to be cared for
seems to cause much despair,
If I could gain feelings I would just love myself,
Just too long for the touch of another,
To not feel so lonely would make my dreams come true,
And turn midnight to sky blue, How
I float when I'm with you,
Just to think of you makes my heart
melt, Wish you felt what felt,
now alone I will drift away and melt…all alone by myself…

Future…

I don't believe we'll be together for eter-
nity by what he said to me,
One little mistake could ruin the whole thing,
So love has no part on if it's just us two,
In the drop of a dime we could be through,
No and's, if's or but's just a simple "I'm through with you"
It cuts like a knife but what can I do,
Say no, don't go if it doesn't work,
Condemning myself to unhappiness if it doesn't work,
Or pick myself up off the ground and brush off the dirt,
Although scarred and pained its okay
to say I would be hurt,
Never the less life goes on and I must
not settle for the dirt….

Not Used Too

Is it too much to ask for something I'm not used to,
Used to waiting up late and him not call-
ing not coming over,
Or texting late with no reply,
Feeling with anger and hurt inside,
Used to crying on my pillow, thinking he doesn't care,
Is it too much, asking for something I'm not used too,
I guess so cause I tell you what he do and
you do the same thing too…

Nightmare...

As the nightmare begins to roll away,
The rain doesn't pour and with dark skies the suns stays,
Speaking into the heart of me,
All things I want to make me free,
Loving not just all earth but also me,
So impeccable and amazing as my mind begins to race,
Through at love lost and push forward and re-
wind to nights alone and nights of cries,
As the nightmare begins to come an end,
I think to myself, have I found a life long friend.

Why

Why doesn't he love me as I love him,
Why doesn't he care for me as I care for him,
Why can't he think of me as much as
I think about him,
Loving him pass life and not seizing to exist,
Maybe he isn't the man for me,
Just a figment of my imagination of what I
want my man to be,
Why doesn't he love me as much as I love him,
Why doesn't he give of himself as much
as I give of me,
Why can't he just love me and want to be free,
Time passing by me as if I idon't exist,
Reflecting upon that last kiss,
Reflecting upon us as if it were only dream,
Maybe this whole being of you was only a
temporary fulfilling dream,
For my heart to be filled with glee,
For my heart to pour out singing,
So now I ask why doesn't he love me,
Why doesn't he love me as I love him,
And want to be with me as I would like to be with him….

When No One Else

WHEN NO ONE ELSE IS THERE,
ALCOHOL ALWAYS SEEMS TO SOOTHE THE PAIN
OR
MAKE IT GO AWAY,
WHEN LOVE SEEMS TO RUN FROM ME AT EVERY
CORNER,
PAIN AND ALCOHOL PUTS MY MIND AT EASE
AND I GO INTO A DEEP SLEEP,
ONLY TO HAVE DREAMS OF PEACE,
UNTIL I AWAKE AND RETURN TO AGONY,
TIL AT LEAST I BEGIN TO HAVE ANOTHER
DRINK, WHEN NO ONE ELSE IS THERE, ALCO-
HOL KEEPS ME COMPANY,
WHETHER IT BE WINE OR VODKA,
IT SOOTHES THE SOUL TEMPORARILY,
JUST LONG ENOUGH TO FAVE THE REALITY,
THAT THINGS NEVER CHANGE ONLY SEASONS
AND THE PEOPLE YOU MEET,
BUT THOSE THAT CLAIM FOREVER ALWAYS
REMAIN THE SAME,
UNCHANGING, UNWANTING AND WANTING?
TO TRADE YOU IN,
BUT ALCOHOL WILL ALWAYS BE YOUR FRIEND
TO THE END,
THE CHURCH SAYS GO TO GOD, BUT IT
DOESN'T
SEEM TO NUMB THE PAIN,
SO I TURN TO MY DRINK AND MY DEEP DOWN

HIDDEN PAIN,
AND I SIT AND DRINK AND CRY UNTIL PAIN HAS COME AND GONE BY COMING DOWN OF THE RAIN,
AND IN THE END I ASK WHAT DID I JUST GAIN,
IF ANYTHING AT, WAS IT MORE THOUGHTS OF NUMBNESS
?THAT I'LL HOPE TO DISAPPEAR,
OR WAS IT HAPPINESS, ONLY TEMPORARILY HERE,
WHEN NO ONE ELSE WAS THERE, IS THERE, OR WILL BE THERE,
I KNOW THIS WILL TO HELP TAKE AWAY THE PAIN,
JUST LONG ENOUGH FOR ME TO COLLECT MY THOUGHTS AND MY HEART BACK I CAN GAIN BACK AGAIN….

Can't Give Up

They say that anger is nothing but hurt,
They might be right because now I sit here crying tears,
Rolling down my face and I'm lost trying to figure out why,
I had no answers so I sat there and cried,
Finally I look at myself in the mirror,
Eyes blood shot red,
In this life I dread,
So I tell myself I am young and strong,
To just hold on,
But my eyes once again tear-up,
So I figure why not just give up,
Because I can't, because I've come way too far,
But in my mind I'm saying this is way too hard,
So I relax and leave a prayer to God….

Untitled

Pain is love and love is pain,
But I loved him so much I
nearly gave my soul,
Cause all I ever wanted was
to be held from the cold,
Kissed in the rain and loved in return,
For an eternity and beyond,
Til all that was left, was time overrun…

Roller Coaster

Sitting upon this roller coaster,
As it goes up, as it goes down,
Makes my head spin all around,
As I try not to let the pressures of
this life be my downfall,
So as I sit I begin to realize that my
life has been up and down,
Been turned in and out, much
like this roller coaster,
That I sit upon but unlike me
it sings the same sad
song day by day,
While I can change my life,
So as I begin to attempt to get out,
it takes me high up in the sky,
I get out only be floating upon some clouds,
But then I begin to feel myself fall-
ing as I snap back into reality,
Working in the kitchen, cleaning everyone's dirty dishes….

You... Thought

You hurt me and you don't care,
Thought you said, you'd always be there,
You hurt me and yet you laugh,
Thought you never wanted to see tears upon my face,
You hurt me and talk behind my back,
Thought you proposed because you wanted us to last,
You hurt me and you don't care,
Thought you'd always be there,
You hurt me and you don't care,
So I'll go pick up a veil instead of crying tears of hell…

Dancing Across

Dancing across the room I look for your face,
And long for your embrace,
Going through the arms of others but
they're nothing like you,
I wish I could turn back time and be the one for you,
Dancing across the dance floor I look out for your face,
Knowing you're the perfect match in this love race,
But I screwed up, so I'm alone, missing you all
day and all night long,
Dancing across the room I wish it was me in your
 arms instead of her,
But I know why that can't be,
So instead of not having you at all,
I'll be the best of a friend that I can be,
Til both of our dreams because bitter sweet reality…

Alone I Love You

Your voice sticks out in my head,
Your cries pierce through my heart,
I know you've given up on me,
But for some reason I still love you,
So I'm stuck trying to figure out if I should tell you,
Seeing that it was me who broke up with you,
I love to love and only want to love you,
I never knew not having you around
would hurt this much,
So when I see you or hear your voice
I enjoy it because,
I've fallen in love with you,
I don't understand why I do the things I do,
Or why I was so mean to you,
But now a lonely spot lies within my heart,
Because for the first time in awhile I can't hold your
smile in my hand,
Feels like all around I'm sinking in quicksand,
Then again alone you feel as I do,
Traveling rocky roads, dealing with love and not
knowing what to do,
You say no one understands you, but I want to,
I want to know everything about you,
The way you feel, what makes you smile
or what gives you chills,
Now I sit alone upon a rock waiting for
you to pass me by,
Hoping I can be a friend and help your life be a
little more than just alright…

A Talk Between A Father And His Lost Child.....

I gave him the best of me and when I went to God on bended knee I wondered what could I give Him seeing that I had already given myself to another man,
I was searching for love that no one on earth could offer me and asked God if He knew someone that could possibly help me,
I went to a man for love and peace and there God stood still by me,
I was hurt by him and cried so many nights trying to figure out if he was right for me and still God stayed and comforted me,
I fell down upon a rock and no man was there to pick me up but God helped me to my feet,
I looked out and behold a beautiful view of blue, pink and yellow and asked God why must, I endure this life of pain and misery alone,
I searched the world for an answer to my prayers and still God stood with me,
I went down to my Father's side and began to ask Him why me? His reply was simple; I have heard your cries and been with you through the tears, been with you when you felt alone, trying to let you know you were not on your own, I have seen you looking for the love of a man and I have always been there with you for you can rest in my hands, for the love I have will fill every void and every

hole you have within your heart, I am your first love and to me you will return and when that earthly love comes and it will come you will know him because he will fill that whole deep in your heart that has been reopened so many times, for it is I alone who mends it each time, when you fell not only did I help you up but I carried you, and when you questioned me I never forsake you and when you wondered what you could do for me, it is simple as to just love me and be ready to understand what that love is for it is not so simple but to know and remember that I will be there the whole while carrying that load right by your side. So never worry nor shall you cry…..
the love of a Father while at His daughter's side….

Realization

REALIZATION HAS NEVER ONCE AP-
PEARED TO ME SO CLEAR, SO BRIGHT,
THE REASON THAT WHY I HATE
FOR YOU TO BE MAD AT ME,
THE REASON I TAKE THE TIME OUT
TO CALL YOU JUST TO SAY HELLO,
THE REASON I LONG TO SEE
YOUR FACE AT LEAST
ONCE A SAY,
REMINISCING ON ALL THE TIMES WE'VE
SHARED AND HOW I WANT YOU IN MANY WAYS,
HOW I THINK OF YOU MORE THAN
I THINK OF ANY OTHER,
HOW I WOULD PUT AWAY CHILD-
ISH GAMES AND PUT MY PHONE ON
MUTE FOR YOU AND ONLY YOU,
REALIZATION HSAS NEVER ONCE AP-
PEARED TO ME SO CLEAR, SO BRIGHT,
IN MY MIND AND OUT OF SIGHT,
GUIDING ME WITH YOUR WORDS, KEEP-
ING YOUR TOUCH IN MY HEART,
DREAMING OF YOU AT NIGHT AS
I LAY AND TRY TO SLEEP,
YOUR VERY EXISTENCE CAPTIVATES MY
MIND AS THERE IS NO OTHER LIKE YOU,
AS I TRY TO PUT MY WORDS INTO PERSPEC-
TIVE I DON'T KNOW HOW TO TELL YOU,
THAT TRULY AS WE BOTH LIVE AND BREATHE
THAT I AM IRREVOCABLY IN LOVE WITH YOU…..

Four Letters:

Love is a four letter word that sends us
into emotional roller coasters,
It makes us toss, makes us turn,
Makes us inside with feelings burn,
It makes us want forever with only one person,
And if something may go wrong the world should flee,
Because we become an unstable wreck
experiencing only sadness,
And saying things that cause more pain,
Not seeing any sunshine and only days of rain

Never:

I never thought in a million years that I could feel so
much pain at once,
This feeling of hurt, anger and a want to cry of release,
Feels like I've been hit by a reality of one that really sucks,
When we speak of eternity and then here
I am again waiting for time to pass,
Not sure of at any moment you'll give up on me and
this won't last,
I never thought in a million years I could feel so much
pain at once,
You asked me if I was mad, the question should've
 been if I felt hurt,
Because it hurts as I sit here trying to hold back the tears,
Knowing that all we spoke of together was years and when
we return from the idea of forever to just being together,
And together never last long enough and for-
ever always means an eternity,
But what second thoughts crossed your mind to
make you not want to when you say that,
You are sure that I'm the one but you be-
gin to think that we're moving to fast,
I ask how could I be so blind as to think
someone would want to marry me,
Let alone to have to be with me for an eternity,
I fooled myself into thinking that this would last forever
because chances are you have someone else in mind,
And I feel so much hurt inside,

I never thought in a million years I would feel so much pain at once,
Never once did I think it would hurt this bad,
Not once did I imagine giving myself to a man as to loose myself in him,
And only care for him as much I want him to care for me,
It was as if I was left standing at the alter upon completion of walking down the aisle,
And breaking down immediately crying tears of pain,
Felt like I was hit and something inside me,
That wasn't me wanted to cause you hurt,
But I'm not one to seek vengeance like that,
So instead of muscle and bone ached at once inside,
Telling myself I would be okay, as I am always,
Picking up my pride from whence I cast it aside,
Never once in a million years did I think
I would feel so much pain at once,
Waiting for the question only to see
if that's how far we'll last,
Never once in a million years,
Never once in a billion years,
Never once in a lifetime,
Never once before like this did I feel so much pain at once,
Now I know how deep love can hurt,
Especially when you call them true love,
Never once in a million years did I think
I would feel so much pain at once,

And the Earth Cries Too

When she cries she thinks,
That no one feels her pain,
She let's out a cry of help and no one comes,
So the earth cries too and wraps her in it's arms,
And suddenly she is alarmed because some-
one is there to comfort her,
And as an outsider, I watch because the earth cries too,
Not just for comfort but because she feels her pain too,
So the earth squeezes and embraces to make her feel safe,
Because she walks the streets and sees no safe haven place,
That mother of her son, she slows and walks alone,
No one feels her pain,
And so the earth cries too,
Because no one could understand that mother crying,
That mother crying because she has no one
and yet the earth is crying too…

He Has Been Good To Me

IT WOULD TAKE EVERYTHING IN ME TO LIE
AND SAY THAT HE HAS NOT BEEN GOOD TO ME,
GOD, THE ONLY FATHER, HOLY
SPIRIT AND TRINITY,
THE DIVINE, THE THREE, THE ONE
WHO HEALS BOTH YOU AND ME,
TRULY IT IS AN HONOR TO SAY THAT
HE HAS BEEN GOOD TO ME,
FORGIVING ME, SETTING ME FREE AND
MAKING THE TRUTH BE KNOWN,
WHEN THE WORLD LETS ME STUM-
BLE OR LETS ME FALL,
HE PICKS ME UP SO ON WEARY DAYS
I DON'T FALL, BUT WALK,
TRULY HE HAS BEEN GOOD TO ME,
THAT'S WHY I MUST THANK HIM FOR
THAT FAVOR THAT SURROUNDS ME,
WHEN I WALK AT NIGHT IN THE
DANGERS OF THE STREET,
THAT'S WHY I MUST TELL THE WORLD
THAT HE'S BEEN GOOD TO ME….

Life

Living the life of the unapologetic,
Hustling in life just to make the bill pay,
Try'na stay out the streets to help my mom with the kids,
Father's never been there or ever gonna be there and
only knows me when he's in a time of need,
I asked for your presence and you gave me broken promises,
That soon was followed by lies,
And if I asked for your help,
You would say I'll see what I can do, not can't make
nay promises and baby girl I love you too,
But I never saw the funds when we lost our home,
Homeless one time, but God lifted me,
To the point that I no longer wanted to hate you,
And that soon became pain and trying to move on again,
Trying to build trust with you,
Just to cry again and again,
Going to with another broken heart
for my mother to mend,
Because she told me she would always be there
for me as a mother and friend til the end….

Real Man:

A real man will love me for me,
Not what I have to offer or what's sacred to me,
But that'll love me for me and only me,
A real man will hold me with no questions asked,
If he claims to know me insides and out,
He'll know to give me a hug from behind,
It's more romantic and it eases my spine,
A real man will not try to buy my love,
But make me happy no matter what,
Because our love is just that strong,
Doesn't ever want to see me upset,
Never ever want to leave me alone, A real man will do what he has to do, taking his time and breaking no rules…

God & Love

NEVER THOUGHT ONCE GRASPING ON TO THE
IDEA OF LONELINESS WOULD LOVE COME FUL-
FORCED AND BE SO REAL AS TO MEND BROKEN
WOUNDS AND FIX BROKEN HEARTS AND HEAL,
TO BRING MUCH JOY, NO HURT, NO PAIN, CAST-
ING ASIDE MANY NIGHTS OF PAIN AND RAIN,
THINKING OF LOVE FULFILL AND PLACED
IN FRONT OF ME BY GOD'S OWN HAND NOT
ONCE, NOT KNOW SINKING IN QUICKSAND,
OF RUSHING OR MOVING TO SLOW OR TO FAST,
KNOWING THAT GOD'S LOVE IS REAL AND WHO
HE SENT ME IT'S GOING TO LAST.....
NEVER THOUGHT LOVE COULD COME SO
STRONG AS TO UNFOLD MANY LIES AND HURTS
AND THINGS OF PAST VOWS,
NOW NOT ONCE THINKING TO GET MY HEAD
OUT OF THE CLOUDS AND COME BACK DOWN
TO EARTH CAUSE THIS LOVE I KNOW IS REAL,
SATAN CAN SEND A FAKE BUT GOD'S LOVE AND
HIS CHOICES ARE ALWAYS TRUE AND REAL,
NOW TIME FUL-FILLS WHAT PROPHETIC WORDS
ONCE CAME FORTH NOT BRINGING BAGGAGE
OR PAIN OR HURT, JUST JOY AND MORE JOY AS
DAYS GO PAST,
COMFORTING AND MENDING SO IN
MY HEART I KNOW IT'LL LAST.....

Even When:

EVEN WHEN SHE THOUGHT HE WOULD SHOW THAT HE CARED,
HE TOSSED IT OUT THE WINDOW APPLYING LITTLE OF HIMSELF,
THOUGHT EVERYTHING WOULD WORK ITSELF OUT,
APPARENTLY NOT SO SHE BEGIN TO WONDER WHAT CAUSED THE DOWNFALL,
LATE NIGHT TALKS AND BOTHERSOME FRIENDS,
THOUGHT MAYBE THEY'D BE TOGETHER TIL THE END,
HOW WRONG WAS SHE TO THINK THAT HE'D BE THE ONE TO PICK HER UP,
SHE CARRIED HIM AS HE CARRIES HER,
THEY CARRY EACH OTHER'S WEIGHT WHEN THE OTHER IS WEAK,
EVEN WHEN SHE THOUGHT HE WOULD SHOW HE CARED UP TIL THE LAST SECOND,
HE LET IT ROLL OFF HIS SHOULDER AS IF SHE OFFENDED HIM,
KNOCKING OUT HER HEART WITH THE LAST WORD THAT HE SPOKE,
AS IF THEY WERE NOTHING BUT SOME CHILD-ISH JOKE,
YET HE THOUGHT THE WHOLE WHILE HE WAS THE ONLY ONE HURTING FROM
THIS THING THEY CALL LOVE,

BUT I THOUGHT IT TOOK TWO, YET SHE'S THE ONLY ONE HURTING THROUGH AND THROUGH,
SEEMS AS IF HE COULD CARELESS, DOING HIS OWN THING MAKING SURE HE PLEASES HIMSELF,
WHILE SHE PUTS ON A FRONT TRYING TO PROVE TO HERSELF THAT SHE'S OK,
TRYING TO MAINTAIN AS SHE PACKS AWAY ANOTHER SET OF MEMORIES,
TELLING HERSELF COLD IS COMING SO YOU HAVE TIME TO PUT YORSELF TOGETHER,
LET IT ROLL OFF AND PUSH FORWARD CAUSE HE DOESN'T CARE,
SO DID HE EVER REALLY CARE,
PUT ON A SHOW POURING OUT HIS HEART,
BUT THEN LET YOU GO AS IF YOU WERE NOTHING BUT A SHOW,
A TEMPORARY FILLING TIL HE FOUND SOMEONE WHO PLEASED HIM,
EVEN AS SHE STARED INTO HIS EYES WITH TEAR DROPS FILLING IN HER EYE,
HE WALKED AWAY AND SAID GOODBYE, THEN CALLED LATER AND SAID GOODNIGHT,
AS IF THEY HAD NOT BEEN THROUGH A FIGHT,
BUT THE NEXT DAY TO HER SURPRISE AS SHE WAITED THINKING,
WAITING FOR HIS RETURN, HE ANSWERED HER WHY,
IT WAS AT THAT MOMENT THAT SHE REALIZED HE NEVER CARED AND SO HE HAD A GREAT

DAY,
WHILE SHE HOPED SHE WOULD SEE HIM AFTER THE WORKDAY WAS OVER,
SHE WAS A FOOL TO BELIEVE THAT THEY WOULD BE FOR ETERNITY,
SHE WAS JUST ANOTHER TROPHY TO PUT UP ON HIS WALL,
BUT IN THE END REALIZING HE CAN'T BE HER DOWNFALL,
SLOWLY SHE PULLS HERSELF TOGETHER MENDING FROM THE HURT AND CLOSING HER HEART ONCE AGAIN,
VOWING NEVER TO BE HURT AGAIN,
IMPOSSIBLE SURE BUT WHY NOT IS WHAT SHE QUESTIONS WHILE SHE PICKS UP HER TEAR DROPS,
EVEN IN THE END SHE STILL ENDED UP HURT,
SO WHEN WILL SHE GET THE POINT OF HURTING NO MORE?
SHE ASKS HERSELF WHILE LOOKING AT PICTURES OF HIM AND HER,
STARTING TODAY AS I BEGIN TO MOVE AT A CHANGE OF PACE,
AND IF I MUST FINISH ON MY OWN THIS THING CALLED A RACE.
SO BE IT ALONE THEN TO FINISH THE PAINFUL LOVE RACE.....

Won't Be Your Fool Anymore...

ONE IN THE MORNING AND I'M TOSSING AND TURNING
LAST TIME CHECK YOU LEFT AT SEVEN, SAYING BABY I LOVE YOU,
BUT I SHOULD'VE KNOWN ABOUT THE GAMES, TELLING ME ALL MEN AREN'T THE SAME AND THAT YOU'RE NOT LIKE THOSE OF MY PAST,
COULD'VE FOOLED ME, HELL I WAS ACTUALLY DOWN FOR YOU,
DOING WHAT I HAD TO DO JUST TO PLEASE YOU,
AND NOW YOU'RE CAUGHT UP WITH ALL THOSE HOES TOO,
SPITTING GAME LEFT AND RIGHT,
SAYING ONE DAY YOU'D BE MY WIFE AND I PROMISE ONLY THEN WILL
EVERYTHING BE ALRIGHT,
BUT WHAT ABOUT THE NOW, THE PRESENT,
YOU WANT TO STAY OUT LATE AND CREEP,
KEEP IT TO YOURSELF AND JUST LET ME BE SO MAYBE THEN I CAN GET SOME SLEEP,
INSTEAD OF TOSSING AND TURNING WORRYING ABOUT YOU,
YOU WENT OUT LATE, YOU BROKE THE RULES,
GET MAD AT ME WHEN I CHANGE WHAT I DO,

GUESS I'LL KEEP HOLDING ON
THE LAST THING PURE I
HAVE WITHIN MYSELF,
THOUGHT YOU WERE WORTH IT,
TURNS OUT YOU'RE JUST LIKE THEM,
THOSE OF MY PAST WHO COULDN'T LAST,
LATE NIGHT PHONE CALLS, CREEPING ON THE LOW,
THINKING SHE A FOOL SO SHE'LL NEVER KNOW,
MAYBE I WAS A FOOL BEFORE, BUT I JUST CAN'T BE YOUR FOOL ANYMORE,
SO DO WHAT YOU DO AND WATCH ME DEPART,
BUT IF EVER YOU'RE IN TROUBLE I'M A PHONE CALL AWAY,
JUST DON'T EXPECT ME TO STAY,
TO BE HURT AGAIN OR TO PUT UP WITH YOUR MESS,
BECAUSE BEFORE YOU EVEN CALL TO ATTEMPT TO BLAME ME,
I'D SAY IT WAS YOUR FAULT, I CAN'T HELP THAT YOU'RE A LOST CAUSE,
DIDN'T KNOW WHAT YOU HAD UNTIL AFTER I LEFT,
BUT NOW YOU HAVE YOUR BEST FREEDOM YET BECAUSE I WON'T BE A FOOL ANYMORE,
BY THE WAY I PACKED YOUR MESS
AND LEFT IT BY THE DOOR.........

Loving You

TRYING TO THINK OF THE ONE IM WITH BUT
CONSTANTLY YOUR NAME POPS IN MY HEAD,
CONSTANTLY I SEE YOUR NAME JUST WALKING
PAST ORDINARY PLACES, SOMETIMES I THINK
MUST THIS LOVE LIFE I DREAD,
TRYING TO SLOW DOWN AND SAY FORGET
ABOUT YOU,
BUT EVERYTIME I DO THERE IS SOMETHING
THAT SURPRISES ME ABOUT YOU,
SO MY FRIENDS SAY I HAVE A BIG ISSUE I SAY NO
AND DUST IT OFF BECAUSE I LOVE MY BOO,
BUT THE ISSUE LIES THAT I THINK OF
YOU WHEN IM WITH HIM AND THE
QUESTION IS WHO AM I LOVING MY
BOO OR AM I LOVING YOU????

As I Reminisce

As I reminisce about our friendship,
Thinking of how far it has went,
And now the way that it is ending,
Life is so, very overwhelming,
As I reminisce about our friendship no longer there,
Thinking of how feelings came about,
And now there is no way to work it out,
No talking no speaking, not even a hi,
I think it's about time to say goodbye,
As I reminisce about our friendship,
Wishing you good luck, both you and your girl,
We don't even talk, we barely have time,
Used to say you was my friend and that one day you would be mine,
As I reminisce about our friendship,
Thinking of the he say and she say that we went through,
Having our boyfriends and girlfriends go through it to,
But I think it's time to say good-bye,
And begin anew....

Miss You

It hurts knowing I won't have you around,
To have and to hold for when I'm down,
I miss you already,
Feels like centuries,
I pray that one day you'll come back to me,
So alone I watch as the sun struggles to come out,
Thinking of you the whole while,
In love we were departed, separated from one another,
I hope my love soon we'll return to one another,
For your touch is as soft as the silk I seek,
And your kiss makes me free above all frees,
And that smile of yours so right,
Like when you hold me nice and tight,
And the love that you pour out,
Too bad the world can't feel it too,
Otherwise they would love you like I do,
I miss you my love, so come back to me soon,
And I hope and pray you'll feel the same too,
Cause not everyday does a love come like you do…

Come Back

All I can do is think about is you and her,
You being in her arms,
Her being in your arms,
And you forget about me,
I probably shouldn't be alarmed,
Me loving you and pictures of you literally loving her,
But I'll love you through it anyway,
Cause my love forever is here to stay,
But just say no matter what you'll come back to me babe…

God's Love Race

I sit and contemplate about going home
with my Father and my life,
That thing that's filled with happi-
ness, some tears and some strife,
As I look around and see the smiles upon everyone's face,
I realize that I miss being in God's love race,
To reach a goal and such a point of faith as I
start something new starting with today,
I begin to remember dancing before throne miss-
ing God's face within this long life storm,
Slowly to return back to the kingdom and remember,
Why I miss His love, because it comforted me and
replaced all hurt that I felt when I was weak,
To see men and women of God and they not
know about my fall makes me want to act on that
for which I was called, Such joy and jubilee,
It's no wonder that they are all free, and stay
bound in the word and maintain strong belief,
To finish God's love race is my strong pas-
sion that will make me free….

Mesmerizing

What do I call this mesmerizing infatuation,
that makes me drop my deepest thoughts to
think of his charm and smile,
He lures me with his eyes that hold such
compassion,
A smile bright enough to make the
darkest rain cloud go away,
And a word so sweet to make all the hurt
go down the drain,
What do I call this mesmerizing glance,
That makes me want to stare and go
into a trance,
That makes me want to just be me
dancing among my bedroom floor and
throughout my dreams,
I look, he looks, and we both begin to smile,
Thinking if only we could stop time,
Maybe our lives would be just fine,
But knowing on happiness we can get by caring for
each other in and out of this lifetime,
What is this mesmerizing, hypnotizing
joy that leaves
my mind racing,
While constantly we are pacing,

And the wonders of the world seeing them with him,
Would be amazing and yet I'm hoping this
is not just a phase,
Or crazy infatuation,
All around in every aspect he is amazing,
And makes me smile with gentle words daily…

Describing Him

How do I describe him?
Sweet and caring,
Wondering about other
Peoples needs as we as
Having a mind that's free,
His ways are all in good intentions,
Hasn't asked for my loyalty,
Or my submission,
Just a life-long friendship,
That's how it all begins,
But with this and his presence
there is no world-wind,
No need to lie, to cheat or sin,
No if's, an's or but's that's
How it all began,
A single card game that taught,
Us each many lessons,
Some fun, some laughter and a new beginning,
The most important thing was not winning,
Just laughter with each other,
So in the end, no one says, oh brother....

He {a man like no other}

He understands me,
Is he the one for me?
Helps me understand this life,
Teaches me prosperity, no strife,
His love surrounds me and chases away nightmares,
He holds my hand when I am scared,
He understands me in and out,
Looks pass my flaws and all defaults,
Grows with me over time,
Fills that void once empty and null,
He gives me strength where I am weak,
He comforts me til I am sleep,
He takes my hand as we pass the bridge,
Encouraging me to look forward and not down,
For He is a man like no other,
He is different for every other person,
He's a father that cares,
He's that's mother that's never been there,
And He always waits for us too return home,
He's awake all day and even as we sleep,
So who is He???
Like I said He is different for both you and me,
He is a man like no other….

I'm Stuck

I'm stuck in life on this thing called love,
Asking if you're the one sent from up above,
While we exchange hateful words,
Is that what you would call love?
We break up to make up and we argue
before we go to sleep,
We go at times without seeing each
Other for weeks,
Yet still we find ourselves
Back to one another saying that
We love each other,
I'm stuck in life on this thing called love,
Not being able to move on from this thing
we call our bond and our love,
Constantly finding myself thinking of you,
And getting mad at the world when I can't see you,
Watching people all around exchanging
I love you's and how do you do's,
Instead I sit and think of how I loved, love and
Will always love you,
I spell your name in the sand as I walk along the beach,
Hell I even dream of your name as I sleep,
I'm stuck in life on this thing called love,
A bond two people share that
Nearly always sent from above when it's not lust,
To be down when the one you love is not around,
To try to move on and still you're stuck on them,
That one person who has kept moving on,
Or so you think til at last your eyes meet…

I Love

I love you more than words can say,
Love your smile, your unique ways,
I love you more than what I thought,
Even through those thoughts I fought and fought,
I love you more through all my fear,
Never to stop you from drying a tear,
I love when your soft hands meet my face,
Shows your sensitivity and caring ways,
Love is a word that cant be tossed around,
But you show me the meaning of true
love from day to day,
You're heaven sent in the most loving way,
I love you more than words can say,
So all I say is I love you babe…

Spend Life With

I look at him and think that's someone I could
spend my life with,
I want to look at him and say that is the one
I want to be with,
But surprisingly I don't that's not the
relationship I want,
Maybe a little more than friendship,
But not too much too handle,
I look at him and think I want
to be with him,
I want to look at him and smile because
of the life we both chose,
And someday he'll see that girl and agree with
the idea of to have and to hold…

Feel through Life

Walking through the memories of hol-
low trees and buried dreams,
Of a life that once crashed by anger and
despite so full of content and overwhelmed by fear,
Holding grudges, not shedding one single tear,
Through all the pain and agony,
Thinking to myself do they understand that some
take life as a game,
And only bring about pain and misery,
Although the might love company,
It cuts as deep as a knife,
And it hurts when its your family or your best friend,
To have and to hold just to be hurt again,
To despise the very person who helped give you
life because they never cared,
Never was there for you,
Thanking God for every breath, you inhale, exhale
while going through hell,
Trying to find meaning in this life some love,
Hate or refuse to experience,
All because of their environment,
Or broken promises that were never gonna be kept,
Telling God thank you anyway in advance for the joy
we have this very day,
With that thought in the back of your mind,
That part of you that wants to break down and
cry on the inside,

Going through life, refusing to shed a tear,
Knowing that it has hurt for many, many years,
But you can't stop running although you
must breakdown,
Upon the finish line as you take home the gold,
Back to that point of to have a to hold,
Until the earth's resting place takes your soul….

Sitting & Thinking...

Sitting and thinking about me and you,
Asking why I think you aren't being true,
Call and there's no answer cause you don't
Pick up the phone,
So then I say don't call so your questions
you don't prolong,
I just want it to be over and done,
While you try to press rewind and then re-run,
It's old, annoying and worrisome,
So I want to let go,
So move on and let it snow,
Still I want you,
As if your words weren't the only thing unreal and untrue,
Your actions in that category too,
So there it is, you have my final words of truth,
I believe you lied, cheated and know
you never had the time,
So now what flows out of this is a sad, simple rhyme…

I Give

I give and give with nothing in return,
Nothing left, not even a grain of strength,
Trying my best to forgive and forget,
But it's too hard, but I don't quit,
I give and give with nothing in return,
Simple I love you's and no meaning behind it,
No peace for my mind,
And I get out Just in time,
Never trying to push rewind,
Never trying to regret,
Trying to tell myself I haven't seen the best yet….

Every Other

He was just like every other,
Mesmerizing eyes, the same nice game,
With sweet lines,
Never once thinking they'd be the same cheap lines,
So soon our hands were intertwined,
Hanging out and he whispers softly in my ear,
Telling me such things as I'll always be there,
Making promises that I would never forget,
Til he broke his word and like the others came
to get what he thought he could get,
He was like every other,
It's just first I couldn't see,
Til that day I could clearly see what
he had turned out to be.

What's It Like...

Will I ever know what it's like to be loved be a man?
One that is not father or a friend?
But one that's gonna stand by my side,
Will I ever know what it's like to be loved by a man?
Not just wanting to be a friend but a lover for all time,
There's a real love for all, so why am I alone,
Will I ever know what it's like to be loved by a man,
For better or for worse?
Til death do us part for all time,
Will I ever know what it's like to be loved by a man?
Will I ever know what it's like just to be loved…..

{Watch}

As I watch other's in love and loving each other,
I realize I'm alone and have met another,
I looked upon the reflection that stares back at me,
Of the eyes that tell a story,
Of anger, hurt, pain, agony, and all the
things that eat her up inside,
No one ever taking the time to realize,
That she's already had love before and
just wants to be loved some more,
To feel complete, to feel whole again,
But she can't because in love she's cursed,
No one to love her more or equally as she loves them,
No one to comfort her as she push-
es away, tears rolling down her face,
She watches them and they watch me,
Never really knowing the deep down agony....

Out The Way

You wanted for me to get out your way,
To go and change your page,
To say single again and I wonder why
did we ever become more than friends,
Never really wanted to be with me,
So why waste my time just joking and
Downing me,
And chasing after other females right
under my feet,
But I guess you never did love me,
And that's okay I know I must stay,
Strong and continue to move on,
Got me out the way now,
You can do what you choose,
Just know as of now, I still love you…

Gave You

I gave you my heart and you walked over it,
Gave you my soul and you tossed it like a piece of cake,
I gave you the best of me and not once
did you consider my needs,
I gave you all of me,
And in the end all I had was me,
I loved you more than I loved myself,
Cause I thought you would stick around
and join me in my wealth,
I cried over you and you saw through me,
And at the end of the day still I used to love you....

Queen For A Hoe

Why is it when you find a queen you let her go for a hoe,
You'd rather it be a breeze or a tease,
And not the configuration of the games you love,
I have what I want is what you say about her,
And yet you still chasing these other girls,
Why do you trade diamonds for pearls,
Both are pure and sweet,
But one carries more luxury,
Instead you go for the one with dusty feet,
Like being interrupted jamming to an old school beat,
The princess, they call beautiful but she's been
broken down so much,
She doesn't know how to love,
Won't let anyone in or let anyone score her love,
Because of the pain or because of the hurt,
And because of everything else that hurt her before…

You

Awesome is a word that I wouldn't use
much to describe anyone,
But you are,
Nice, caring, sensitive,
All the things that's real,
My broken heart you can heal,
For you have started to mend
The strings that my heart cling to,
And now I know I want to be with you,
My heart is heavy, now these burdens I life too,
When I see you or spend time with you,
I melt inside at the thoughts of you,
That flow through my mind,
I love you more than I love time,
You're great and wonderful all around,
No need for me to walk around
with my head down,
All tears washed away when true
love was found….

Nobody

Nobody sees her pain,
Feels her pain or knows her pain like I do,
She's always smiling, joking and laugh-
ing and pretending everything is alright,
Until Friday or Saturday nights,
Oh yeah is all she thinks as she prepares for the club scene,
Going out with my girls and feeling my swag
is what she says on her myspace page,
No one knows exactly what she means so
the think she's okay,
Her boyfriend doesn't notice her change in
appetite or the way she feels,
He knows her story but not the way she feels
it or how it plays over and over in her mind,
Her story of pain, hurt, heartache, tears and screams,
No one hears in her silent screams within her dreams,
No one knows her pain like I do,
No one knows because the girl and I are only
one and not two....

Playing With Love

Some play with love as if it's just another four letter word,
Telling it to every female they meet,
Never taking it seriously,
Toss it like a salad and into the garbage
like trash but it's fine,
I should've known it wouldn't last,
Some take love for granted,
A gift that'll always be there,
Til you see her with someone else,
And now you're all alone by yourself,
You're stare hoping she'll stare back and gaze
into her future's eyes and his to hers,
And now you think of what could've, should've
and would've been,
If you had of kept her within your grasp,
Instead of always leaving her alone,
And turning your back for you your boys,
Some don't understand what it means to love,
So instead when they use love it only brings
about hurt and they are the only ones left
crying within the dirt…

Thinking

Thinking of time,
Thinking of you and I,
Wondering if we'll be together for eternity,
Loving your smile, loving every moment and
baby that's not it,
Seeing you walk, seeing you dance,
Picture me and you together just holding hands,
Dancing to a nice song of romance,
Thinking of me,
Seeing us together walking through trees,
I'm singing to you,
You singing to me,
We both go together like honey and bees,
You make me free gazing into your eyes,
You make me smile,
thinking of you throughout the day,
And I just think of us forever throughout the days….

Feel What I Feel

THEY WILL NEVER KNOW WHAT
IT IS TO FEEL WHAT I FEEL,
THEY DONT KNOW THAT WHAT I FEEL IS REAL,
THEY DONT UNDERSTAND THAT I
AM IN LOVE WITH THIS MAN,
SO WONDERFUL SO TRUE,
PICKS ME UP WHEN I AM FEELING BLUE,
THEY DONT KNOW HOW HE MAKES
ME FEEL INSIDE AND OUT,
MAKES ME FEEL REAL GOOD SHOWING
ME THAT HIS FEELINGS TO ARE REAL,
HE SAYS WILL YOU TAKE ME AS YOUR MAN,
YOUR KNIGHT AND SHINING ARMOR,
I SAY YES AND HE BEGINS TO KISS ME FROM THE
HEELS OF MY FEET TO THE NECK OF MY SPINE,
 AND I THINK OH MY GOD THE WHOLE WHILE,
THEY DONT KNOW HOW HE MAKES ME FEEL,
ITS THIS RUSH OF ADRENA-
LINE THIS CRY OUT OF JOY,
 A THING CALLED LOVE THAT
MY SOUL LONGS FOR,
WHAT AN EXPERIENCE,
WHAT AN EYE OPENER TO FEEL
WHAT I FEEL KNOWING NO TEMP-
TATIONS JUST ADMIRATION,
 HE BRINGS OUT THE BEST OF ME
SO YES IF HE ASKED I WOULD LET
HIM GET THE BEST OF ME.......

Fool

RIGHT BACK AT POINT A WHERE I WAS BEFORE,
BEING HURT AND ALONE WITH-
OUT AN EVEN SCORE,
I POUR OUT MYSELF AND AGAIN IM LEFT
STANDING LOOKING LIKE A FOOL,
WHILE I TELL MYSELF TO STOP
THINKING ABOUT YOU,
STOP TELLING YOU HOW I FEEL BECAUSE
I WILL END FEELING LIKE A FOOL,
TELLING YOU THAT I ALMOST LOVE YOU, WHY
THAT WOULD BE STUPID OF ME TO DO,
BECAUSE AS I SIT AND FIGHT TRYING TO
GET YOU OFF MY MIND YOU WILL NEVER
UNDERSTAND SO I WILL ONLY BE HEAR-
ING THE SAME OL SAD RHYME,
BUT I SAY WITHIN MYSELF I REFUSE
TO LOOK LIKE A FOOL THIS TIME.

I Wonder

I wonder what you think when you look into my eyes,
Because you say such sweet things to my surprise,
Your hands are so soft and your smile amazing,
Like when you begin to part your lips and say
things that cause me to sway in my ways,
Looking into your beautiful eyes all I can say is oh my,
To be graced with such a man at the likes of you,
never forgetting the things you say or do,
I think I find a romantic of you,
While you bring my inner being out,
The person no one sees,
Simply because you see pass the surface of me,
Of all my flaws and all and taken time to say
I'm thinking of you,
And I think to myself will his ways be true,
Sure he's amazing through and through,
Late night talks before I sleep,
Bringing about a certain tranquility of peace…

Love You More

I love you more then you love me.
I love you in a way that makes us both more than free,
I love you more than you love me,
my love for surpasses all trees,
it passes mountain tops and pass all oceans of seas,
I love you more than you love me,
Passs endless barracks, pass endless soldiers in military greens,
I love you more than you love me and always will for eternity....

Gifts

To write, to dance, to sing and shout,
Are not gifts of the world,
But gifts of the masters hands,
The creativity that flows in and out of our minds,
Like still I rise, still we rise and let's all of us rise,
Are not just words of endurance, perseverance, and determination,
That tell a story of how we as a society have risen from nothing,
To many some things and some bodies,
And still we grow for it is not on our own,
It's part of the master's plan,
So some of us thank him in advance,
To tell a story, practice fundamentals and use such things as techniques,
Didn't just come from the idea of you and me,
So why do we practice this society of the idea of me and only me,
When we have not been born of ourselves and live not by controlling our own lives and breathe,
Life was in His plan, in His hands, even when we think that we control society,
The gift to speak, hear and see are not from the idea of me, me and oh yes me,
But of His plan, His idea, His thoughts of a life containing both you and me,
So together we can stand and live in unity…

How Can??

How can you say you love me,
And you choose your boys over me,
When they don't care about your happiness,
And only want to see you continue to run the streets,
How can you say you love me,
And you'd rather spend time with them,
Than pinking up the phone making a two minute call,
And say I'm tripping and yet there's no fall,
How can you say you love me,
When you no longer care,
Only care when you're here and not when you're there,
How can you say you love me,
And you won't change,
Telling your friends you got me hooked and that
I'll always return,
How can you say you love me,
And you place your boys above me,
When I thought only I could hold you night,
And only I was the one of your dreams that
could meet your needs.
So how can you say you love,
I'm dying to know,
How could you love me and mot let your past go????

I Love You,..

I love you, tis this is true,
I love you through and through,
I love you this I know within my heart,
I always loved you,
Right from the start,
I love you,
More than I can say,
I love you each and everyday….

Take my heart

You take my heart and tear it apart,
Said you loved me from loves first start,
Since then we've been inseparable,
Growing in love and then growing apart,
Growing together to be together for as long as we live,
Loving each other because that's the way we want to live,
Giving each other what's necessary to live,
You take my heart and mend it some days,
Making me sometimes sway in my way,
Growing with you like growing with my music,
Growing with you like growing with trees, growing with you as you are my perfect melody,
When you want to be,
You take my heart and hold it in your hands,
so I ask myself what is in today's plans???

Woman To Woman

WOMAN TO WOMAN AS A WRITER
I CAN UNDERSTAND YOUR POINTS
AND UNDERSTAND YOUR VIEWS,
FEEL HOW YOU WOULD FEEL HURT
AND THEN AGAIN BE CONFUSED,
WOMAN TO WOMAN IF I WERE YOU I
WOULDN'T KNOW WHAT TO SAY OR DO,
BUT AS A WOMAN I MUST SAY THAT
I HAVE BEEN IN YOUR SHOES,
WOMAN TO WOMAN I THINK
LOVE IS EVERYTHING TO ME,
HAVING MR.RIGHT AND KNOW-
ING MANY MR.WRONGS,
FINDING THE KING TO TAKE ME AS HIS QUEEN,
AND LOVING ME FOR ME AND ONLY ME,
WOMAN TO WOMAN I MUST SAY I
CAN FEEL WHAT YOU FEEL,
EXPRESSING YOURSELF IN LITTLE WORDS AND
FEELING BOTH HURT AND HAPPINESS INSIDE,
WOMAN TO WOMAN I SAY THIS LAY-
ING ASIDE MY PRIDE,
BECAUSE IF I'M TO BE APART OF HIS LIFE
THEN I MUST BE APART OF YOURS SO,
WOMAN TO WOMAN I MEAN TO BRING
NO ANGER, PAIN OR WRONG,
KNOWING HOW IT FEELS TO LOVE SOME-
ONE AND THEM NOT LOVE YOU,
WOMAN TO WOMAN FROM A WOMAN'S POINT

OF VIEW BEING CONTEMPT IN ALL THAT I DO,
CAUSING NO STRESS OR DRA-
MA BETWEEN ME AND YOU,
LETTING YOU KNOW I RESPECT
YOU AND ALL THAT YOU DO,
WOMAN TO WOMAN IT'S NOT EASY HAV-
ING KIDS BY SOMEONE YOU'RE NOT WITH,
BUT WOMAN TO WOMAN YOU'VE
FOUND YOUR KING AND SO HAVE I,
SO EXCUSE ME IF I FEEL NO NEED TO APOL-
OGIZE FOR WHAT I'M ABOUT TO SAY,
LOVING HIM IS ALL THAT I INTEND TO DO FOR
THE REST OF MY LIFE AND ALWAYS BEING TRUE,
NO MATTER WHAT THE WORLD
SEES OR THINKS OF HIM AND I,
HOPING WE'LL BE TOGETH-
ER IN AND OUT OF TIME,
WOMAN TO WOMAN I CAN FEEL YOUR PAIN,
BUT WOMAN TO WOMAN I HAVE
SEEN MANY DAYS OF RAIN,
BEING ALONE AND LONELY HAVING NO
ONE TO HOLD ME AND LOVE ME FOR ME,
STEPPING ON MY HEART AS YOU
FEEL HE HAS DONE YOURS,
HE MEANS NO HARM AND KNOWING HIM
HE'S SORRY IF YOU FEEL THAT WAY,
CAUSE I LOVE HIM AS HE LOVES ME
AND I'LL BE THE FIRST TO SAY I'M HAP-
PY YOU FOUND YOUR KING,
WOMAN TO WOMAN I MEAN
TO CROSS NO LINES,

MEETING YOU ONE DAY WHEN IT'S
THE RIGHT AND PROPER TIME,
SO WOMAN TO WOMAN BE HAPPY AND
NEVER LET LOVE GO WHEN YOU FIND THAT
KING THAT FUL-FILLS YOUR EVERY NEED,
CAUSE EVERY QUEEN NEEDS A KING
TO LOVE HER FOR A ETERNITY,
WOMAN TO WOMAN I'M HERE WITH
NO DRAMA OR STRINGS ATTACHED,
CAUSE WOMAN TO WOMAN ALL WOMEN
ARE MORE THAN JUST PAIN AND MISERY,
WE'RE LOVE AND PEACE AND EVERY-
THING THAT A MAN NEEDS TO BE
MADE WHOLE AND COMPLETE,
GIVING EACH OTHER UNCONDITIONAL LOVE
AND FUL-FILLING ONE ANOTHER'S NEEDS,
SO WOMAN TO WOMAN WE ARE
WHO WE CHOOSE TO BE,
WOMAN TO WOMAN I'M HERE FOR-
EVER AND AN ETERNITY HOLD-
ING NO GRUDGES OR ANGER,
JUST BEING THE WOMAN MY
MAN NEEDS ME TO BE,
WOMAN TO WOMAN IS ALL WE HAVE TO BE,
CAUSE I'M NOT TRYING TO TAKE YOUR PLACE,
I'M ONLY TRYING TO LOVE
HIM AS HE LOVES ME,
SO WOMAN TO WOMAN IS ALL
THAT WE NEED TO BE…

I Love You

I love you because you are everything I've ever wanted and so much more,
I love you because you are you nothing less in which I adore,
I love you because you're kind and caring and not in any way about you,
I love because you know what's in my heart before I even tell you,
I love you because you're wonderful and nothing of you I want to change,
I love you because you're awesome and you're understanding in ways I've never seen,
I love you because you make promises that I know won't just be a dream,
I love you because in this short time you've made me feel completely rejuvenated and whole,
Nevertheless opening your warm heart to mine of cold,
I love you because I can trust you and know that your word you'll keep,
I don't know why I feel the way I do but I know that deep inside above all else I love you,
I love you because you've begun to mend my heart and not by buying gifts or taking me out but just for being there,
Being there like no one else has and always reminding me that you care,

I love you because you're you and no one else can compare,
To the way you treat me and talk to me and let me know you appreciate the things I do, no matter what it is that I may or may not do,
I love you simply for just being you cause money can't buy happiness but it sure can bring about pain and I know how you are and no pain are you ever willing to bring,
I love you.........

We Go Back

We go back like peanut butter and jelly,
My first real kiss,
My first real love,
My first of many things,
Like my first best friend,
Everybody wanted you and swore you were heaven sent,
We go back like white rice and gravy,
You were my one only true female best friend,
No matter how far apart we were,
You were always there,
Through rainy nights and hard times,
And even when I was scared,
Encouraging me throughout those marches and telling me I had potential when you fell under my leadership,
Still we go back,
Like when home alone and the little rascals first
Came out,
Fighting with me to toughen me up,
Being as much of a friend to me as I was to you,
Now we're both grown and still thick as thieves too,
Now us, we go way back,
You were there for me when I came out of the womb,
Covering up my scratches and scars,
Taking me in and telling me it'll be okay,

You knew I was sensitive so you was strict on my play,
Knew he wasn't there and still said
there will be a brighter day,
Said I'd be great one day if I stayed in
God's will and never went astray,
Yes, as I reminisce we all go way, way back in the day…
We go back…

Through & Through

Through winter's cool breeze,
Through spring and summer's rains,
Through life's agonizing pain,
I love you,
Through arrogant people I encounter,
Through Korea's harsh winter,
Through speechless cries and midnight blues,
I love you,
Through pain from years before,
Through doors closed and opened doors,
Through maledictions harmonies,
I love you,
Through and through, I love you….

Love For You

Midnight days and sunlit nights
The peak of peaks of a roller coasters heights,
The love I have for you extends pass a rockets flights,
Long less nights of pitch black midnight,
Starry eyes and starry days,
Days of life and college haze,
The love I have for you extends pass rainfall days,
Midnight days and sunlit nights,
Mountains of high and rivers of low ,
Living without you through days of cold,
My love for you extends pass to have and to hold,
Extends pass this life I declare so bold…

You Would Rather...

You would rather see me fall,
Than to see me lifted up,
To see me hurt and scorch inside,
Than to say I'm sorry because of your pride,
You would rather see me fall,
Than to see me be exalted pass you,
Go pass his head so that I don't surpass you,
You would rather see me fall,
Than to succeed, knowing my dreams are becoming reality,
And nothing positive about me comes out of your mouth,
Just endless negativity,
I'm sorry Mrs. I'm just not afraid to be me,
And stand up for what I believe in,
Not afraid to be my own woman and stand up for me....

Back To The Streets…

It was nice to know that you went home
and fell out of love with me,
Being around old habits and old friends
and slowly you forgot about us,
No longer wanting to be in love,
And you told me you wouldn't change,
Club hopping, show stopping and running the streets til dawn,
No phone calls and no thoughts came
across your mind of me,
As you were to busy doing your thing in the streets,
While I waited for you to show that you loved me,
And only dreamt of you as I slept,
Wanting to be in your arms,
Wanting to hear your voice,
Through rough times and life's storms,
I was selfless for you,
Giving you my last dime,
If only I could go back and turn the hands of time,
I would've never met you,
And I would've never said yes to proposal after proposal,
Because you would not have been worth the time,
If I knew you would go home for a month
and just drop me like I was a dime,
No, I don't regret the whole four months
of our time in summer months,
This distance between you and me creates much agony,
As I begin to see to see there is no you and me,
As you have left me to return back to your selfish ways and to return back to the streets…

Fall's Changes

Fall's changes makes us open our eyes,
To realize how life takes us by surprise,
Realizing how you never loved me,
Never once was I the root to your tree,
Falls changes makes us open our eyes,
To realizations that might cause us to mesmerize,
No loner wanting a partner to watch the sunrise,
Falls changes makes us open our eyes,
To remind us of how the summer brought good times,
And winter brings heartache and pain,
And although how there's no rain,
It feels like storm clouds anyway,
Falls changes makes us open our eyes to things
that never were,
That makes us want to cry,
Sometimes it makes us want to hide,
Alone from the rays of the sunlight,
Or instead run into the darkness if night,
Falls changes makes us open our eyes.
To change all around in the midst of
life's unwilling crown…

End of Ends

I'll love you til the end of ends,
I'll miss you more than I miss sin,
Trust my love will never quit,
Trust me with your heart and I'll be good to it,
Trust me with your soul and I will cherish it,
I'll love you til the end of ends,
Breaking your heart and then making amends,
Trying to repair and never break again,
As we remember the old but let it go to begin,
I'll love you til the end of ends,
I'll love you always no matter where or if we ever end....

360

You change 360 and say everything's my fault,
I take the blame, expecting that for our rela-
tionship, maybe we should both change,
Listening to your boys and me listening to my heart,
never knowing that we're both going two different ways,
Now my heart tells me,
To remain calm and things will change,
But I know for the better part of my mind that they won't,
So I continue this hunt for love but still I'm wanting you,
Because you changed 360,
And say I called it through,
By going crazy because I missed,
So yeah, if the world wants to know,
I emailed you because I missed you,
And then I got hurt when I didn't hear back from you,
Or what sense does it make to read a message
and not reply, not one word, not even a hi,
What sense does it make to know that I called,
And not once pick up the phone or hit redial,
Because you turned 360,
When you got around old habits,
I take the blame and not it's after 12,
Because you wanted to know who called,
But it wasn't on your phone,
So why does it matter,
Yeah, sure we talk but it's not like you want too,
You only want to point the finger and take
none of the blame on yourself,

Because I emailed you, because I missed you,
And so I cursed you out because I hadn't heard from you,
And instead of talking to me,
You believe all the people you think have your back,
When most of them look my way and ask about you,
And see you aren't there so try to fill you shoe,
Even though I told them that I only wanted you,
And yet you believe them,
Because you turned 360,
When you went home,
So sure I took the blame,
Because I thought of all people at least
you would want to work it out,
Guess I was wrong and so how fast you move along,
Because you turned 360,
I took the blame,
And now I'm thinking to myself to
love I must really be insane….

No More

No more us,
No more one,
No more of you rising before the sun,
I gladly take the blame,
Though it wasn't all my fault,
And still you depart,
No more playing til midnight,
No more thinking til dawn,
Cause you took my heart away,
And in the sand is where you left it to stay,
And I admit that I apologize,
But must I pay for this my whole life,
No more us,
No more one,
No more of us rising together before the sun,
I say I love you,
You press forward pass you and me,
No more talks of I want to marry you,
Because your love ran out,
When you boarded the plane,
And now I am forced to feel the wrath of my own pain,
No more us,
No more one,
No more rising before the sun,
No more us,
No more one,
No more rising together before dawn…..

Will You Care???

If you loose me, will you care?
If I don't to be there and you want to be near me,
will it bother you?
If you know that I still love you and don't
nothing to say to you,
Will you care or just go and get another girl and
eventually trade her in too?
If you loose me, will you care?
If I take my heart from you,
Will it mean anything to you?
If you, knowing in all your heart and
I told you that I loved you,
If I walk out that door, will you stop me or just
let me pass through,
Do you love me too,
Do you really love me as much as I love you,
If you loose me will you care,
If I gave you my heart and left it with you there,
Can I come back to find it still the same and unchanged of,
Will I come back to something gone forever in the dust,
Leaving no residue, not even a scuff,
Or can I find it safely stored with your heart,
Because you still care for me,
Or like all others, do you too set my heart free,
If you begin to loose me will you care,
Only time will tell, when we come back to ourselves…

Every Dude

Every dude always says let me love you,
And that they'll be good to me,
So I try to give my all and only love you for you,
Enduring hardships and some hurtful words from you,
But still through it all I managed to love you,
Even when the clock rolls around midnight twice,
And not once did I hear your voice
three midnights since flights,
Every dude always says let me love you,
But I want to know can you handle my hurt from times before if I begin think you're gonna walk out the door,
Can you handle the fact that I might be paranoid,
Because my own father didn't want apart of me,
Can you handle my hurt or just add too,
If I give you my heart and all my soul too,
Can you handle the love I'll have for you,
Can you handle, how much I just might miss you,
Every dude says, let me love you,
But at the end of the night when I need you most,
Will you be there, to see me through???

Take Back

Take back the ring,
Take back the before,
Take back all those things you said before you closed the door,
Take back your "I love you's"
Take back the wedding vows containing I do,
Take back your kind words and just leave me hurt,
Take back it was really nice to meet,
Take back the I want to be with you,
Take back your heart and give me mine,
Take all this back with a twist of time,
Take back all the late night phone calls,
Take back everything and leave me on the court,
Exactly where you met me, just as before,
Take back the I fell in love with you,
Take back all those things,
Because none of them where ever true,
Take back all of it because true love never gives up,
Take back all of it and leave as is,
Take back all your lies,
Take back all your love,
Because it just wasn't real enough,
So take it all back,
And no mistake in my mind,
When you take it all back,
Never come back in my life,
So take it back and leave me as I am,
I can make it by myself,
I'll make it because I can….

Your Voice

I call my voicemail just to hear your voice,
I call you just to talk to you,
I write about you just to be near you,
I hold you in my heart and don't know why,
I used to love you,
I used to be with you,
I used to know you more than I do,
I call my voicemail just to hear your voice,
To hear you speak, til I'm asleep,
Just hear you,
Just to be near you,
Just to feel remotely close to you,
Just to feel safe with you,
I call my voicemail just to hear your voice,
I call you just to talk to you,
For hours at a time or time elapses,
Thinking about love as my heartbeat fastens,
As our thought clashes,
Thinking and speaking on love and other things,
Causing my heart to increase in speed,
I call my voicemail just to hear your voice,
Just feel close to you,
Replaying the message you left because
it makes me smile,

Knowing you wanted to talk,
Knowing you still love me,
Knowing that you want to be no matter
what are my insecurities,
Makes me happy, makes me smile,
So I call you just to talk a little while,
Just to hear you and fall in love with you,
I call you just to hear your voice,
I call my voicemail just to hear you,
Because deep inside I miss you too…

I Am

I am deeper than what you know,
I am deeper that what you see,
I am grounded by the one who grounds all trees,
I have a praise in me I don't know how to maintain,
I have a joy inside that won't just let me be,
I am filled by the one who makes all rivers flow,
To make all light in darkness glow and show,
I am deeper than what you know....

LaVergne, TN USA
29 October 2010

202737LV00003B/38/P